Chips for Tom Revolution Unveiled

Inside the Battle for Superiority Between Nvidia, AMD, and Intel, and the Future They're Shaping

Rick A. Kruger

Copyright

© 2024 by [Rick A. Kruger]

All rights reserved. No part of this book may be reproduced, stored in a retrieval system, or transmitted in any form or by any means, electronic, mechanical, photocopying, recording, or otherwise, without the prior written permission of the publisher.

Table of Contents

CHAPTER 1 15

   AI CHIPS' ASCENT 15

      Early Computer and AI History 15

      Evolution from General-Purpose Computing to Specialized AI Chips 16

      Role of GPUs in AI Development 18

      AI's Transition from Gaming 20

      Early Advancements and the Development of Generative AI 24

CHAPTER 2 30

   NVIDIA'S DOMINANCE 30

      Nvidia's Breakthrough with Blackwell 30

      Market Impact and Industry Response 32

      Introducing Rubin: The Future of AI Chips ... 34

      The Role of GPUs, the New Vera CPU, and Networking Chips 36

      Jensen Huang's Vision and Roadmap for the Future .. 37

      Strategic Moves and Market Position 39

CHAPTER 3 46

   AMD'S CHALLENGE 46

AMD's AI Evolution 46

Key Milestones and Product Launches 48

The MI300X and Beyond 50

Lisa Su's Strategic Roadmap: MI325X, MI350, and MI400 52

Competitive Strategy and Market Impact 54

Innovations and Advancements in AMD's AI Chips .. 56

CHAPTER 4 61

INTEL'S ENTRY INTO THE AI ARENA 61

Intel's Legacy in Computing 61

Historical Significance of Intel in the CPU Market 62

Transition to AI and New Product Lines 63

Arrow Lake and Future Prospects 65

Patrick Gelsinger's Vision and Strategic Outlook 68

Intel's Competitive Strategy 70

Innovations and Collaborations in AI Development .. 73

CHAPTER 5 76

THE TAIWANESE CONNECTION 76

Significance of Taiwan in the Tech Industry 76

Taiwan's Role as a Hub for Semiconductor Manufacturing 78

Key Events and Trade Shows: Computex 80

Cultural and Familial Ties 81

The Unique Connection Between Nvidia's Jensen Huang and AMD's Lisa Su 83

Impact of Their Leadership on Their Respective Companies 84

Chapter 6 90

   THE MARKET DYNAMICS 90

      Investor Reactions and Market Trends 90

      Stock Market Responses to New Product Announcements 90

      Analysis of Market Share and Sales Figures 93

      Global Demand for AI Chips 96

      Generative AI Applications 97

      Projections for Future Demand and Market Growth ..98

CHAPTER 7 103

   TECHNOLOGICAL INNOVATIONS 103

      Advancements in AI Chip Technology 103

Key Technological Breakthroughs by Nvidia, AMD, and Intel 103

Future Directions and Emerging Technologies 108

Impact on AI and Computing 110

How These Advancements Will Shape the Future of AI and Computing 112

Potential Applications and Industries Affected 115

CHAPTER 8 120

  CHALLENGES AND OPPORTUNITIES 120

    Competitive Pressures 120

    Nvidia: The Market Leader 120

    AMD: The Challenger 122

    Intel: The Veteran 123

    Impact of Global Trade Policies 125

    Supply Chain Disruptions 127

    Strategies for Mitigating Risks and Ensuring Stability 128

CONCLUSION 133

  THE FUTURE OF AI CHIPS 133

INTRODUCTION

A technological revolution has been triggered by the emergence of artificial intelligence (AI), which is changing industries and pushing the boundaries of computing power. AI chips, the specialized processors powering the complex algorithms driving AI applications, are at the center of this revolution. These chips serve as the foundation for both current and upcoming technological developments in addition to being the heart of sophisticated computer systems. The competition between the top three chip makers—Intel, AMD, and Nvidia—intensifies as demand for AI capabilities rises, with each vying for market share, performance, and innovation. These IT behemoths' recent debuts in Taiwan, which highlight their most current innovations and pave the way for further breakthroughs, represent a turning point in the AI chip market.

An Overview of the Industry for AI Chips

Within the larger semiconductor business, the AI chip industry is a quickly developing sector that is distinguished by intense rivalry and constant innovation. Artificial intelligence (AI) chips are made to tackle the demanding computing workloads needed for AI applications like large-scale data analysis, machine learning, and neural network processing. AI chips, which are typically in the form of GPUs (Graphics Processing Units), TPUs (Tensor Processing Units), and other specialized accelerators, are optimized for parallel processing, which is crucial for handling the intricate calculations involved in AI workloads. In contrast, general-purpose CPUs (Central Processing Units) are not designed for parallel processing.

AI chips are important for reasons more than just their technical specifications. They play a crucial role in facilitating AI-driven developments in some industries, including robotics, natural language processing, autonomous cars, and medical diagnostics. These chips are a focus of research and development because of their performance and efficiency, which have a direct bearing on the viability and efficacy of AI applications.

An Overview of AI Chips and Their Importance

In today's computer world, AI chips—which are made expressly to speed up AI computations—have become essential. These chips are significant because of their capacity for massively parallel processing, which is essential for developing and implementing AI models. Because of their sequential processing-optimized architecture, traditional CPUs are not well suited for such tasks. GPUs and other AI accelerators, on the other hand, are designed to manage thousands of simultaneous operations, which makes them perfect for the data-intensive and iterative processes that characterize workloads in artificial intelligence.

AI chips enhance the performance of AI systems by reducing the time required to train models and execute inferencing tasks. This capability is vital for applications that demand real-time processing, such as autonomous driving and interactive AI assistants. Furthermore, the efficiency of AI chips translates to lower energy consumption and operational costs, which is particularly important for large-scale data centers that run AI applications around the clock.

The influence of AI chips on the economy is significant. The need for high-performance AI chips has increased dramatically as companies from a variety of industries use AI technology to obtain a competitive edge. The increase in demand for AI chips has resulted in substantial investments in research and development, which has accelerated breakthroughs and fueled ongoing efforts to create designs that are more potent and efficient. In addition to being a technological competition, the race to create the greatest AI processors is also a geopolitical struggle for market supremacy and financial power.

Brief History of the Major Players: Nvidia, AMD, Intel

Three major players dominate the AI chip market: AMD, Intel, and Nvidia. With a long history, all of these businesses have been essential to the advancement of computing technology.

NVidia

When Jensen Huang, Chris Malachowsky, and Curtis Priem formed Nvidia in 1993, their primary focus was on graphics processing units (GPUs) for the gaming industry. Due to its exceptional graphical performance, the company's GeForce series of GPUs completely changed the gaming business. But Nvidia's entry into AI started when it realized that its GPUs' parallel processing powers were ideally adapted to the computing needs of deep learning and artificial intelligence.

A parallel computing platform and application programming interface (API) called CUDA (Compute Unified Device Architecture) was unveiled by Nvidia in 2006, enabling programmers to take advantage of GPU capabilities for general-purpose computation. The foundation for Nvidia's supremacy in the AI chip market was established by this invention. Subsequent releases from the business, including the Ampere and Volta architectures, cemented its leadership in AI acceleration.

Nvidia's 2019 acquisition of Mellanox Technologies, which improved its capabilities in high-performance computing and data center networking, further demonstrated the company's strategic focus on AI. Some of the most sophisticated AI systems in use today are powered by GPUs from Nvidia, and the business is always pushing the limits of AI chip efficiency and performance.

AMD

Advanced Micro Devices (AMD) was founded in 1969 by Jerry Sanders and seven colleagues from Fairchild Semiconductor. AMD initially produced logic chips and later expanded into microprocessors. For much of its history, AMD has been recognized for its rivalry with Intel in the CPU market. However, like Nvidia, AMD also identified the potential of GPUs in the AI landscape.

AMD entered the GPU industry in 2006 when it acquired ATI Technologies. Gamers took to the company's Radeon series of GPUs, but AMD's emphasis on heterogeneous computing—combining CPUs and GPUs on a single chip—paved the way for its aspirations in artificial intelligence. With an emphasis on AI and machine learning applications, AMD's ROCm (Radeon Open Compute) platform was unveiled in 2016 and offered an open ecosystem for GPU computing.

AMD has rejuvenated its product selection and recovered competitiveness in the CPU and GPU industries under the direction of CEO Lisa Su. The MI50 and MI60 are the first in the company's MI (Machine Intelligence) series of accelerators that are specifically developed for AI workloads. With the MI300X and upcoming devices, AMD has demonstrated its dedication to maintaining an annual release schedule, underscoring its resolve to disrupt Nvidia's hegemony in the AI chip industry.

Intel

Founded by Gordon Moore and Robert Noyce in 1968, Intel is one of the most illustrious businesses in the semiconductor sector. Intel's x86 microprocessor design established the company's supremacy in the CPU business and became the industry standard for personal computers. But compared to Nvidia and AMD, Intel took longer to make the transition to hardware designed specifically for AI.

Intel has taken many calculated steps to improve its standing in the AI chip industry as a result of its increased recognition of the significance of AI. The addition of cutting-edge AI acceleration technology to Intel's portfolio came from the acquisitions of Nervana Systems in 2016 and Habana Labs in 2019. While the company's Movidius line of visual processing units (VPUs) targets edge AI applications, Intel has upgraded the AI capabilities of its Xeon processors, which are generally utilized in data centers.

Lately, Intel has concentrated on developing an all-encompassing AI ecosystem that integrates CPUs, GPUs, and specialist AI accelerators. With the upcoming Arrow Lake CPUs, Intel is showing that it is still committed to competing in the AI chip market. These CPUs are meant to provide great performance for AI and other demanding tasks. Under CEO Patrick Gelsinger, Intel wants to confront its rivals and reclaim its footing by utilizing its vast manufacturing capabilities and resources.

The Importance of the Launches from Taiwan

The recent introduction of next-generation AI chips in Taiwan by AMD, Intel, and Nvidia is noteworthy for some reasons. An essential node in the global semiconductor supply chain is Taiwan, which is home to some of the top producers of semiconductors in the world, such as TSMC (Taiwan Semiconductor Manufacturing Company). The nation's contribution to the production of cutting-edge chips for a variety of applications, including data centers and consumer devices, highlights how important it is.

Appropriate Time and Place

It was a calculated move on the part of Nvidia, AMD, and Intel to introduce their newest AI chips in Taiwan. The annual Computex technology trade expo, which takes place in Taipei, is one of the biggest and most significant gatherings for the sector. It gives businesses a global stage on which to present their inventions and establish connections with important parties, such as investors, journalists, and industry partners. These businesses optimize their visibility and impact by timing their announcements with Computex, demonstrating to a worldwide audience their strategic priorities and leadership in technology.

Technological Progress and Its Effect on the Market

The debuts in Taiwan demonstrate how quickly technology is advancing in the AI chip sector. Nvidia's Rubin platform represents the state-of-the-art in AI chip design, AMD's MI325X accelerator, and Intel's Arrow Lake CPUs, which have novel designs, increased performance, and expanded capabilities. These developments are essential for fulfilling the ever-increasing requirements of AI applications, which call for ever-higher efficiency and computational capacity.

Also clearly visible are the dynamics of competition between AMD, Intel, and Nvidia. Companies compete to show off their technological prowess and gain a bigger piece of the lucrative AI chip industry. The competition spurs innovation, requiring each business to create more sophisticated and effective goods. This rivalry produces more potent and affordable AI solutions, which help not only the companies involved but also the industry at large and end consumers.

Implications for Geopolitics and the Economy

Technology and commercial concerns are not the only reasons why the Taiwan launches are significant. Geopolitics and the economy are closely related to the global semiconductor sector. The worldwide supply chain depends heavily on Taiwan's capacity to manufacture semiconductors, so any disruptions might have a significant impact. Securing dependable sources of cutting-edge chips has become more crucial in light of the COVID-19 pandemic's influence on supply chains and the ongoing tensions between the United States and China.

Nvidia, AMD, and Intel are reiterating the significance of the region in their strategic intentions by introducing their most recent AI chips in Taiwan. These introductions also demonstrate their reliance on Taiwan's manufacturing capabilities to generate high-tech chips on a large scale. These businesses' collaborations with Taiwanese producers like TSMC are essential to preserving their competitive advantage and satisfying the demand for AI chips around the world.

Prospects and Challenges

The AI chip industry's future trajectory was established by the launches in Taiwan. The declaration by Nvidia of a "one-year rhythm" for new chip launches demonstrates their dedication to quick product development cycles and ongoing innovation. Similar to AMD, Intel is keeping up with market demands and technological improvements through the development of its upcoming Arrow Lake CPUs and an annual release cadence.

But there are obstacles in the way of success. The supply chain restrictions, rising R&D expenses, and the requirement for sustainable and energy-efficient designs are some of the challenges facing the AI chip business. Furthermore, Nvidia, AMD, and Intel's fierce rivalry mean that each company must strike a balance between innovation, strategic investments, and market placement.

AI applications are still evolving, which brings with it both potential and challenges. The need for specialized and adaptable AI chips will only increase as AI is incorporated into more areas of business and daily life. Emerging trends like edge computing, AI-driven automation, and the confluence of AI with other technologies like 5G and quantum computing will require businesses to predict and adapt.

In summary

The AI chip industry stands at the forefront of technological innovation, driven by the relentless pursuit of performance and efficiency by leading companies like Nvidia, AMD, and Intel. The recent launches in Taiwan underscore the critical role of AI chips in shaping the future of computing and highlight the strategic importance of the region in the global semiconductor supply chain. As these companies continue to push the boundaries of what is possible with AI chips, the industry is poised for transformative growth and profound impacts on technology, the economy, and society.

CHAPTER 1

AI CHIPS' ASCENT

Early Computer and AI History

The development of devices intended for general-purpose tasks typified the early days of computing. Punch cards and vacuum tubes were the primary components of these massive, room-filling early computers, like the ENIAC and UNIVAC. Although their computing capacity was constrained by modern standards, they established the foundation for the digital era.

During this time, the concept of artificial intelligence (AI) also began to take shape. John McCarthy originally used the term "Artificial Intelligence" in 1956 at the Dartmouth Conference, when the concept of building machines that might mimic human intelligence was initially put out. Rule-based systems and symbolic approaches, which need substantial processing power, were the main topics of early AI research. The constraints of modern hardware prevented these systems from fully encoding human knowledge and reasoning into algorithms.

In the 1980s and 1990s, AI research began to incorporate statistical methods and machine learning, driven by increasing computational power and the availability of more data. These methods required even more powerful computers, pushing the development of specialized hardware. However, it wasn't until the 21st century that AI research would find a powerful ally in an unexpected place: the world of computer graphics.

Evolution from General-Purpose Computing to Specialized AI Chips

For many years, the central component of computing was the general-purpose CPU (Central Processing Unit). They were built to be capable of doing everything from basic math to intricate data processing. But as AI's requirements increased, it became evident that CPUs weren't necessarily the best instrument for the job. CPUs found it difficult to deliver the enormous computational capacity and parallel processing capabilities needed for the development of AI algorithms, especially those requiring deep learning.

The investigation of specialized hardware for AI resulted from this insight. Application-Specific Integrated Circuits (ASICs) and Field-Programmable Gate Arrays (FPGAs) were two of the earliest customized chips made to speed up particular computational activities. ASICs were very efficient for some activities but were not as flexible as FPGAs, whose circuitry could be reprogrammed for other functions. In the field of AI, these developments signaled the start of the transition from general-purpose to specialized computing.

However, the use of Graphics Processing Units (GPUs) for AI tasks was the true breakthrough. Although elaborate graphics for video games were the original purpose of GPU development, several AI algorithms found that GPU architecture was well suited for parallel processing. GPUs feature thousands of tiny cores intended for parallel activities, in contrast to CPUs, which have a few cores geared for sequential processing. Because of this, they were perfect for managing the massive matrix multiplications and convolutions required for deep learning.

Role of GPUs in AI Development

The role of GPUs in AI development cannot be overstated. The shift began in the mid-2000s when researchers started leveraging GPUs for scientific computing tasks. The parallel processing capabilities of GPUs made them perfect for accelerating the computationally intensive operations required in deep learning.

Nvidia, a business that gained notoriety in the gaming sector for its formidable GPUs, saw early on the possibilities of its technology for artificial intelligence. With the release of CUDA (Compute Unified Device Architecture) in 2006, Nvidia enabled developers to leverage their GPUs for general-purpose processing with the introduction of a parallel computing platform and programming style. Researchers may now more easily use GPU power for a variety of applications, including AI, thanks to CUDA.

GPUs had a huge impact on AI research. With GPUs, deep neural network training that might take weeks on CPUs might be finished in a matter of days or even hours. This quickening created new opportunities for AI study and advancement. Due to time and resource constraints, complex models that were previously unfeasible to train became feasible.

In 2012, a group of academics from the University of Toronto led by Geoffrey Hinton utilized GPUs to train a deep neural network known as AlexNet, marking one of the turning points in the history of GPU use for AI. On the computer vision benchmark, the ImageNet Large Scale Visual Recognition Challenge, AlexNet attained previously unheard-of levels of accuracy. AlexNet's accomplishment served as a demonstration of the capabilities of GPUs and deep learning, generating a lot of attention and funding for the topic.

AI's Transition from Gaming

The two leading companies in the GPU market, Nvidia and AMD, first established their brands thanks to the gaming performance of their products. To generate the intricate visual effects and high-resolution images required by contemporary video games, GPUs were necessary. But when GPUs' promise for AI became clear, both businesses had to change their approaches to take advantage of this brand-new, quickly expanding market.

The Shift at Nvidia

Nvidia jumped at the chance to profit from the AI growth. The business was at the forefront of the AI revolution with the release of CUDA and the success of GPUs in AI research. The preferred hardware for academics and businesses creating AI technology is now Nvidia's GPUs.

Nvidia realized that even more specialized hardware was required, so it created the Tesla series of GPUs with scientific computing and artificial intelligence in mind. These GPUs were designed with AI researchers' needs in mind, providing improved performance and functionality. Additionally, Nvidia made significant software development investments, building frameworks and libraries like cuDNN (CUDA Deep Neural Network library) to maximize the performance of deep learning workloads on their technology.

The work Nvidia did paid off. Globally, research labs and data centers have come to rely on the company's GPUs. Prominent digital corporations such as Google, Facebook, and Amazon have embraced Nvidia GPUs for their artificial intelligence workloads. AI became a key growth engine for Nvidia, resulting in a sharp increase in the company's market share and revenue.

AMD's Shift

AMD, the primary rival of Nvidia in the GPU industry, acknowledged the increasing significance of AI. Even though Nvidia got off to a head start, AMD started working harder to get a piece of the AI business. AMD's GPUs, which were renowned for their competitive gaming performance, were also excellent choices for AI applications.

AMD concentrated on improving the GPUs' capabilities and performance for AI applications.

The Radeon Instinct range was created by the business with AI and machine learning workloads in mind. These GPUs supported well-known AI frameworks and provided high-performance computing capabilities.

AMD also placed a strong emphasis on cross-platform interoperability and open-source software. The business advertised an open software platform for GPU computing called ROCm (Radeon Open Compute). The goal of ROCm was to give programmers working on AI and other high-performance computing applications a flexible and scalable environment.

In the AI processor industry, AMD's efforts helped establish it as a formidable contender, despite Nvidia's continued dominance. Numerous businesses and academic institutions began using the company's GPUs, which broadened the range of hardware choices available for AI development.

Early Advancements and the Development of Generative AI

The use of GPUs and the creation of specialized AI hardware resulted in several innovations that revolutionized the industry. Deep learning, a branch of machine learning that makes use of multi-layered neural networks, has become a potent method for a variety of AI applications, such as generative models, natural language processing, and picture and audio recognition.

Speech and Image Recognition

Image recognition was one of the first applications of deep learning with GPU acceleration to be successful. The efficacy of deep neural networks for this task was proven by AlexNet's achievement in 2012. AlexNet was followed by a string of progressively complex models that pushed the limits of image recognition, including VGG, ResNet, and Inception.

By using GPUs, researchers were able to train these intricate models on enormous datasets, leading to great accuracy and the development of new applications. Deep learning-powered image identification systems have become essential to many sectors, including security, entertainment, and the automobile and healthcare industries.

Deep learning also transformed speech recognition. Deep neural networks were used by companies like Microsoft, Baidu, and Google to construct sophisticated speech recognition systems. These solutions performed better than conventional methods, allowing for more precise and organic interactions with other voice-activated devices, such as AI assistants.

Natural Language Interpretation

Deep learning and GPU acceleration also led to notable advances in natural language processing (NLP). Newer NLP systems were built on top of recurrent neural networks (RNNs) and subsequently transformer models.

A significant advancement was made in 2017 when Vaswani et al. introduced the transformer model. Transformers performed remarkably well on a variety of NLP tasks because of their capacity to manage long-range dependencies and parallel processing. Models like BERT (Bidirectional Encoder Representations from Transformers) and GPT (Generative Pre-trained Transformer), which broke previous records for language production and interpretation, were developed as a result of this architecture.

Artificial Intelligence

The field of generative AI, which concentrates on producing original content, has seen a rise in interest and advancement. After being presented by Ian Goodfellow in 2014, generative adversarial networks, or GANs, gained popularity as a framework for producing lifelike photos, videos, and other kinds of data. A generator and a discriminator, two neural networks that compete with one another to produce data of higher quality, make up a GAN.

Variational autoencoders (VAEs) and generative models such as GANs have created new avenues for creativity and invention. Applications for them ranged from entertainment and the arts to scientific research and data enhancement.

Advanced language models that can produce writing that resembles that of a person have also been developed as a result of the rise of generative AI. Large-scale language models can produce text that is coherent and contextually relevant, as shown by OpenAI's GPT series, which culminated in GPT-3. This demonstration sparked considerable attention and commercial applications.

In summary

The emergence of AI processors heralds a revolution in computer history. The desire for more processing power and efficiency has spurred the development of AI from the early days of symbolic AI and general-purpose computers to the present day with the rise of deep learning and sophisticated hardware. Created for gaming, GPUs are now essential to the development of AI, allowing advances in generative AI, natural language processing, picture and audio recognition, and more.

Using their knowledge of GPUs, Nvidia, and AMD have been instrumental in this development. Nvidia established itself as a market leader in AI chips thanks to the creation of CUDA and its early embrace of AI applications. Despite its original concentration on gaming, AMD has made notable advancements in AI hardware.

The need for specialized hardware will only increase as AI develops. GPUs and other specialized chips are at the forefront of a revolution that will reshape the future as AI and faster computing come together. The development of AI chips is a narrative of technological innovation, but it's also a monument to the never-ending search for advancement in the field of artificial intelligence.

CHAPTER 2

NVIDIA'S DOMINANCE

Nvidia's Breakthrough with Blackwell

Development and Features of the Blackwell Chip

The Blackwell chip from Nvidia marks a substantial advancement in computation and artificial intelligence. Blackwell, which debuted in March 2024, has garnered much praise for being the "world's most powerful chip." This chip, which bears the name David Blackwell in honor of the famous mathematician, represents Nvidia's dedication to expanding the frontiers of AI technology.

Blackwell's creation took several years to complete and involved a lot of research and development. The engineers at Nvidia concentrated on improving scalability, performance, and efficiency to meet the growing needs of AI applications. Blackwell's architecture, which blends an unparalleled number of transistors to produce remarkable processing power and energy efficiency, is crucial to its excellence. This is important for data centers since heat dissipation and electricity consumption are important considerations.

The Blackwell chip's capacity to execute parallel computing at a scale never before possible is one of its most notable characteristics. Its sophisticated graphics processing units (GPUs), which are built to handle large datasets and intricate algorithms necessary for AI and machine learning jobs, make this possible. Blackwell also has the most recent tensor cores from Nvidia, which greatly improves AI inference and training performance. The foundation of neural network computations, matrix operations, are the focus of these tensor cores, which are specialized processing units.

Additionally, Blackwell presents an improved memory architecture that includes high-bandwidth memory (HBM), which enables quick access to and processing of data. Throughput is increased and latency is reduced, both of which are essential for real-time AI applications. Another noteworthy advancement in the chip is its interconnect technology, which allows for smooth communication between several GPUs and improves the efficiency of large-scale AI models.

Market Impact and Industry Response

The introduction of Blackwell had a profound impact on the market and the industry at large. Data centers, cloud service providers, and AI-driven enterprises quickly adopted the chip, leveraging its superior performance to enhance their services and products. The chip's launch catalyzed a wave of upgrades across various sectors, from healthcare and finance to autonomous vehicles and robotics.

Following the news of Blackwell, Nvidia's stock price spiked, indicating investor confidence in the company's ability to maintain its position as the industry leader in AI chips. The chip's powers were lauded by analysts, who predicted that it would rule the AI space for many years to come. As a result of learning about Blackwell's technological capabilities, rival companies like AMD and Intel accelerated their research efforts.

An explosion of alliances and teamwork was another aspect of the industry's reaction. As more businesses looked to include Blackwell in their AI frameworks, Nvidia's ecosystem grew. As a result, hardware and software engineers came to have a mutually beneficial partnership that encouraged growth and innovation. Adoption of the chip was not restricted to big businesses; its capabilities also benefited startups and research institutes, democratizing access to state-of-the-art AI technology.

Introducing Rubin: The Future of AI Chips

Features and Advancements of the Rubin Platform

Building on Blackwell's success, Nvidia unveiled Rubin, a next-generation AI chip platform that will go on sale in 2026. This platform, named for the trailblazing astronomer Vera Rubin, is poised to completely transform AI computing in the future. Rubin is a comprehensive update that includes networking chips, CPUs, and GPUs.

Scalability and energy efficiency are prioritized in the architecture of the GPUs used in the Rubin platform, which aim to provide performance never seen before. These GPUs are even more capable of handling sophisticated AI workloads since they integrate the most recent developments in tensor core technology. Even more parallelism is supported by the design, which makes processing large-scale AI models more effective.

The Vera CPU is a major upgrade to the Rubin platform. This new central processing unit offers a strong basis for applications requiring a lot of data because it is specifically designed for AI operations. With the smooth integration of the Vera CPU and Rubin's GPUs, a coherent system that optimizes performance and reduces latency is created. Because of its high throughput and low power consumption, it is perfect for edge computing and data center applications.

Another essential component of the Rubin platform is its advanced networking components. By enabling high-speed data transfer between components, these chips guarantee that the system can manage the enormous data flows typical of artificial intelligence applications. For distributed AI models, which necessitate effective communication across numerous nodes, this networking feature is essential.

The Role of GPUs, the New Vera CPU, and Networking Chips

The interaction of GPUs, the Vera CPU, and networking chips is critical in the Rubin platform. GPUs continue to be the mainstays of parallel computing, thriving in jobs like intricate simulations and deep learning model training. They are essential for contemporary AI applications because of their architecture, which is designed to handle the enormous volumes of data involved in these processes.

To support the GPUs, the Vera CPU controls data flow and performs sequential processing tasks. Its architecture, which includes features like sophisticated cache management and power-efficient cores, is tailored for AI tasks. This frees up the CPU to manage control flows and memory operations while coordinating AI tasks and assigning parallel processing jobs to the GPUs.

The Rubin platform's networking chips make sure that information may move between various system components swiftly and effectively. For distributed AI systems, where data must be shared across several GPUs and CPUs, this is especially crucial. These networking chips' cutting-edge connection technology maximizes bandwidth and reduces latency, allowing for smooth communication inside the AI framework.

Jensen Huang's Vision and Roadmap for the Future

The CEO of Nvidia, Jensen Huang, has been instrumental in advancing the company's ambition for artificial intelligence in computers. His innovative spirit and strategic vision have put Nvidia at the forefront of the AI revolution. Huang has big plans for the Rubin platform, wanting to build an all-encompassing ecosystem that can meet the many requirements of AI applications.

Huang's idea of accelerated computing, which combines high-performance computing and artificial intelligence to tackle the most difficult computational tasks, is at the core of his vision. In Huang's future, artificial intelligence will permeate every facet of computing, from edge devices to data centers. The Rubin platform, which will supply the hardware underpinnings for AI-driven breakthroughs, is intended to be a cornerstone of this future.

For Nvidia, Huang has outlined a "one-year rhythm" for the release of new semiconductors. This ambitious schedule demonstrates Nvidia's dedication to remaining one step ahead of the competition and consistently expanding the realm of AI computing possibilities. Nvidia wants to stay ahead of the technology curve and be able to quickly adjust to the changing needs of the AI business, which is why it releases new products every year.

Strategic Moves and Market Position

Nvidia's Market Share and Investor Confidence

Investor confidence and Nvidia's significant market share both attest to the company's dominance in the AI chip space. Due to its leadership and the broad use of its products, the business accounts for about 70% of sales of AI semiconductors. Nvidia's unwavering innovation and capacity to provide cutting-edge technology that satisfies the demands of a quickly expanding industry serve as the foundation for its success.

Nvidia's solid financial results and strategic direction support investor trust in the business. Nvidia's stock has increased significantly since the Blackwell and Rubin platforms were announced, fueled by expectations for steady growth and market leadership. The ability of Nvidia's technology to influence computing and artificial intelligence in the future is acknowledged by analysts and investors alike, which increases their optimism about the company's future.

Strategies to Maintain Dominance in the AI Chip Market

To maintain its dominance in the AI chip market, Nvidia employs a multifaceted strategy that includes technological innovation, strategic partnerships, and market expansion.

Technological Innovation:

Nvidia's strategy is centered on its unwavering attention to innovation. The business makes significant R&D investments to be at the forefront of AI technology. By consistently enhancing the capabilities, performance, and efficiency of its chips, Nvidia makes sure that it is the go-to option for AI applications. Huang's roadmap, which outlines the yearly release of new semiconductor platforms, helps

Nvidia stay ahead of the competition and react rapidly to market demands.

Strategic Partnerships:

Crucial to Nvidia's approach are partnerships with leading technological companies, academic institutions, and other businesses. With these alliances, Nvidia is able to include its chips into a larger ecosystem of artificial intelligence products, ranging from cloud services to software frameworks. Through tight collaboration with major AI companies, Nvidia can guarantee broad adoption of its technology and application-specific optimization. These partnerships also encourage creativity and propel the creation of fresh applications for Nvidia's CPUs.

Market Expansion:

Nvidia keeps growing its market share by focusing on new markets and uses for its AI technology. The company has successfully expanded its portfolio to encompass data centers, automotive, healthcare, and other industries, despite having first garnered notoriety in the gaming sector. This diversification creates new revenue streams and reduces the dangers connected to depending too much on one market. Nvidia's capacity to handle a broad range of applications prepares it for ongoing development as AI technology becomes more and more commonplace.

Ecosystem Development:

As part of its approach, Nvidia is also creating a strong ecosystem for its AI chips. This covers software tools, libraries, and frameworks in addition to hardware that makes it easier to create and implement AI applications. For example, Nvidia's CUDA platform has established itself as a standard for GPU computing, allowing developers to fully utilize Nvidia technology. Nvidia guarantees that its clients may fully utilize the capabilities of its processors by offering extensive support and resources, which promotes adherence and sustained involvement.

Talent Acquisition and Retention:

Another crucial component of Nvidia's approach is attracting and keeping elite talent. To spearhead its innovation efforts, the corporation looks to the best brains in computer science, engineering, and artificial intelligence. Talented individuals are drawn to Nvidia because of its culture of excellence and dedication to cutting-edge research. Nvidia makes sure it has the know-how required to stay ahead in the fiercely competitive AI chip business by investing in its personnel.

Global Reach:

As part of its global strategy, Nvidia is increasing its presence in important international markets. The business has made a significant impact across continents including Asia, Europe, and North America, concentrating especially on developing nations where the use of AI is growing. Nvidia may seize fresh chances and propel worldwide expansion by customizing its goods and services to meet the unique requirements of various geographical areas.

Nvidia's steadfast dedication to innovation, strategic vision, and capacity to adjust to the rapidly changing technological landscape have led to its domination in the AI chip market. With the introduction of the Blackwell chip, Nvidia established itself as a pioneer in AI computing and raised the bar for performance and efficiency. With the launch of the Rubin platform, Nvidia's leadership will be strengthened and even more cutting-edge capabilities will be available.

Nvidia's commitment to ongoing development and staying ahead of the competition is demonstrated by Jensen Huang's vision for accelerated computing and a yearly schedule for product releases. Through the utilization of technology, strategic alliances, and market expansion, Nvidia is positioned to sustain its leadership and mold AI and computers for many years to come.

Nvidia's position as an industry leader and innovator will be crucial to the advancement of the AI revolution as it unfolds. Nvidia will continue to lead the way in revolutionizing how we interact with and profit from artificial intelligence thanks to its strategic decisions, solid market position, and investor trust.

CHAPTER 3

AMD'S CHALLENGE

AMD's AI Evolution

The transition from Gaming GPUs to AI Accelerators

As a prominent player in the graphics processing unit (GPU) market for a considerable amount of time, Advanced Micro Devices, Inc. (AMD) mainly provides strong graphics cards with high frame rates and the ability to generate complex visuals for the gaming community. But as artificial intelligence (AI) technology developed and its uses grew, AMD realized it would have to change course and focus on AI accelerators, which would completely change its product line and market positioning.

Originally, professional graphics programs and gaming were the main uses for AMD's GPUs. These

GPUs were designed with real-time complex scene rendering in mind, which is essential for high-end gaming and professional graphic design. But these GPUs' architecture also made them appropriate for parallel processing jobs, which is a fundamental need for workloads including artificial intelligence and machine learning.

The need for technology with the capacity to process large amounts of data in parallel increased as artificial intelligence (AI) gained popularity, especially with the emergence of deep learning and neural networks. Because they process information sequentially, traditional central processing units (CPUs) were inefficient for these kinds of jobs. With thousands of cores that can handle several tasks at once, GPUs have become the preferred hardware for AI practitioners and researchers.

AMD started modifying its GPU architecture to better meet the demands of AI applications after realizing this change. This required increasing its

GPUs' computing capacity, power efficiency, and optimization for the kinds of operations typical of AI workloads. To facilitate AI applications, AMD also made software development investments. These included building tools and libraries that made it simpler for developers to use AMD hardware for machine learning and AI applications.

Key Milestones and Product Launches

AMD has established its position in this cutthroat industry with some significant product launches and milestones throughout its entry into the AI accelerator market. The launch of the Radeon Instinct series in 2016 was one of the first notable actions. AMD formally entered the AI industry with these GPUs, which were specifically built for deep learning, inference, and other AI applications.

Many Radeon Instinct models, including the MI25, were built using AMD's Vega architecture. Due to their excellent efficiency and performance, these

GPUs were appropriate for AI jobs including both inference and training. For example, the MI25 boasted 24.6 TFLOPS of single-precision performance—a noteworthy number that put it on par with products from Nvidia, the industry leader in AI GPUs at the time.

AMD kept improving and broadening its product range after the release of the Radeon Instinct series. An important development was the 2018 release of the Radeon Instinct MI50 and MI60. These GPUs provided considerably greater performance and efficiency and were based on the 7nm Vega architecture. For example, the MI60 allowed double-precision calculations and provided up to 29.5 TFLOPS of single-precision performance, making it appropriate for a broader spectrum of workloads related to AI and science.

Strategic alliances and cooperative efforts supplemented these product releases. To incorporate its GPUs into AI infrastructures, AMD collaborated extensively with leading IT firms, academic institutions, and cloud service providers. This showed AMD's hardware's potential in practical applications and helped the company gain headway in the AI business.

The MI300X and Beyond

Features of the MI300X and Its Market Reception

The 2023 release of the Radeon Instinct MI300X signaled a major advancement in AMD's AI hardware capabilities. The MI300X was created to surpass its predecessors' capabilities by providing outstanding performance, efficiency, and adaptability for AI tasks. It stood out in the crowded market for AI accelerators thanks to the inclusion of multiple cutting-edge capabilities.

The improved computational capabilities of the MI300X were one of its most notable characteristics. With a significant increase in compute units, it was able to do more simultaneous parallel processes. Because huge parallelism is crucial for performance in deep learning tasks, like as training and inference, this made it extremely effective. The MI300X also included enhanced memory bandwidth and capacity as well as sophisticated memory architecture. This was essential for managing complicated models and big datasets, which are frequent in AI applications.

Additionally, the MI300X significantly increased power efficiency. AMD optimized the power consumption of the MI300X, making it more efficient than earlier versions, by utilizing its experience in chip design and production. This was crucial for large-scale deployments like data centers, where cooling and power consumption are critical factors.

The MI300X was met with extraordinarily positive market feedback. Reviewers and industry analysts commended its effectiveness and performance, pointing out that it provided a strong substitute for

Nvidia's products. The MI300X was a compelling option for enterprises wishing to develop or modernize their AI infrastructure because of its affordable price and robust performance-per-watt metrics. The MI300X was swiftly embraced by significant data centers and cloud service providers, confirming its capabilities and bolstering AMD's standing in the AI space.

Lisa Su's Strategic Roadmap: MI325X, MI350, and MI400

For its AI hardware segment, AMD outlined a bold strategic plan under CEO Lisa Su's direction. Su revealed a range of next-generation AI accelerators that would keep pushing the limits of efficiency and performance, building on the success of the MI300X. The MI325X, MI350, and MI400 were on this roadmap; they were all notable improvements over their predecessors.

Anticipated for delivery in 2024, the MI325X was engineered to expand upon the framework established by the MI300X. It included more improvements to power efficiency, memory size, and computational performance. The MI325X is a strong option for AI applications that require both high performance and energy efficiency since AMD's developers optimized the architecture to give even higher performance-per-watt.

AMD intended to ship the MI350 in 2025, after the MI325X. Many ground-breaking advancements, including a new microarchitecture that would provide a significant performance boost, were anticipated to be introduced with this model. Additionally, the MI350 was supposed to include cutting-edge machine learning accelerators made expressly to improve the efficiency of AI tasks. The MI350 would become an extremely useful tool for AI practitioners with these accelerators, allowing for quicker training times and more effective inference.

Looking ahead, AMD's vision for AI hardware was embodied in the MI400, which is scheduled for introduction in 2026. The most recent developments in semiconductor technology, such as next-generation process nodes and sophisticated packaging methods, were anticipated to be incorporated into the MI400. With these developments, AMD would be able to provide previously unheard-of levels of efficiency and performance, establishing the MI400 as the industry leader in AI accelerators.

Competitive Strategy and Market Impact

AMD's Approach to Capturing Market Share from Nvidia

In addition to advancing and improving its AI hardware products, AMD adopted a calculated strategy to overtake Nvidia, the industry leader in AI accelerators. Several crucial components were included in this plan, such as aggressive marketing, strategic alliances, and product differentiation.

AMD used performance and efficiency as two of its main differentiators from Nvidia in its product line. AMD sought to provide strong substitutes for Nvidia's GPUs by concentrating on improving the performance-per-watt of their AI accelerators. For data centers and cloud service providers, where power usage and cooling expenses are significant factors, this was especially crucial. AMD positioned its devices as affordable and effective options for AI workloads by providing great performance with little power consumption.

A further essential element of AMD's competitive strategy was its formation of strategic partnerships. The business collaborated extensively with well-known cloud service providers to include their AI accelerators in their infrastructure, including Microsoft Azure and Amazon Web Services (AWS). Through these alliances, AMD was able to establish itself in the market and show off the practical uses of its hardware. Moreover, AMD worked with top academic institutions and AI experts to improve their hardware for a variety of AI uses.

AMD's strategy included strong branding and marketing initiatives. The business made significant marketing investments to showcase the effectiveness, affordability, and performance of its AI gear. AMD used trade exhibitions, conferences, and industry events to highlight its most recent technologies and raise awareness among prospective clients. Through these initiatives, AMD was able to increase its visibility in the AI sector and draw attention from businesses considering investments in AI infrastructure.

Innovations and Advancements in AMD's AI Chips

AMD's success in the cutthroat AI accelerator industry can be attributed to its dedication to innovation and hardware improvement in AI. The business has made constant investments in R&D to expand the capabilities of AI chips, leading to a number of significant breakthroughs and developments.

Chip architecture has been one of the most innovative fields. The engineers at AMD have concentrated on creating architectures that are ideal for AI workloads, integrating capabilities like cutting-edge machine learning accelerators, fast memory, and effective data transport methods. Because of these architectural advancements, AMD's AI processors are able to provide outstanding performance and efficiency, which makes them ideal for a variety of AI applications.

The field of process technology has seen notable progress as well. AMD has continuously improved the effectiveness and performance of its AI chips by utilizing the most recent techniques in semiconductor fabrication. AMD is able to fit more transistors into its processors because to the shift to smaller process nodes, such 7nm and 5nm, which results in improved performance and reduced power consumption. AMD has also looked into cutting-edge packaging strategies including 3D stacking and chiplet designs to boost the effectiveness and performance of its AI accelerators.

AMD has made software development investments in addition to hardware advancements to enable its AI chips. The business has created an extensive collection of software tools and libraries that facilitate developers' use of AMD technology for AI applications. This includes making well-known machine learning frameworks—like PyTorch and TensorFlow—run more smoothly on AMD GPUs. AMD has made it simpler for businesses to deploy its AI technology and incorporate it into their current workflows by offering strong software support.

In addition to producing high-performance AI chips, AMD has established itself as a respectable and competitive participant in the market for AI accelerators thanks to its emphasis on innovation and improvement. AMD's continued dedication to pushing the limits of AI chip technology will be crucial to the company's ability to gain market share and spur future growth as the demand for AI hardware rises.

AMD's transformation from a producer of gaming GPUs to a dominant force in the AI accelerator market is evidence of its capacity for innovation and adaptation in a sector that is changing quickly. Using deliberate expenditures in R&D, an emphasis on efficiency and performance, and tactical collaborations, AMD has established itself as a formidable rival of Nvidia within the AI hardware domain.

Radeon Instinct MI300X and the MI325X, MI350, and MI400 are just a few of the AI accelerators in

AMD's roadmap that show the company is dedicated to pushing the limits of AI hardware. Major cloud service providers and data centers have adopted these solutions due to their excellent market reception and exceptional performance and efficiency.

In the highly competitive AI accelerator market, AMD has been able to gain market share and propel growth because of Lisa Su's leadership strategic vision, and execution. AMD's sustained dedication to innovation and progress will be essential to preserving its competitive advantage and achieving long-term success in the AI sector as the market for AI hardware grows.

CHAPTER 4

INTEL'S ENTRY INTO THE AI ARENA

Intel's Legacy in Computing

Founded by Gordon Moore and Robert Noyce in 1968, Intel Corporation is among the most significant businesses in computer history. Intel, well-known for its microprocessors, has led the semiconductor industry's advancements that have molded the current state of technology. The firm has a long history in the CPU industry, having created some of the most recognizable processors for use in servers, personal computers, and a wide range of other devices.

Historical Significance of Intel in the CPU Market

When Intel released the Intel 4004, the first microprocessor ever made, in 1971, the company's journey in the CPU market officially began. A new age in computing began with this invention, which made it possible to create computers that were more compact, potent, and reasonably priced. Intel kept pushing the limits of semiconductor technology after the 4004 was successful. In 1978, the company released the 8086 microprocessors, which served as the basis for the x86 architecture. For many years to come, the x86 architecture would rule the personal computer industry, making Intel the industry leader in CPU production.

Intel's Pentium processors gained widespread recognition as the benchmark for high-performance computing during the 1980s and 1990s. Since the Pentium brand was introduced in 1993, processing power and efficiency have significantly increased, making it a popular option for both consumers and companies. Because of its unwavering commitment to innovation, superior manufacturing, and strategic alliances, Intel has been able to sustain a competitive advantage and propel the global adoption of personal computers.

In the early 2000s, Intel continued to innovate with the release of multi-core processors, which significantly enhanced the performance of computers by allowing multiple tasks to be processed simultaneously. The Core and Xeon series of processors, introduced in the mid-2000s, further solidified Intel's dominance in the CPU market, catering to a wide range of applications from consumer laptops to enterprise servers.

Transition to AI and New Product Lines

With the increasing demand for applications using artificial intelligence (AI) and machine learning (ML),

Intel realized it needed to expand the range of products it offered beyond conventional CPUs. For the semiconductor business, the emergence of big data, cloud computing, and AI-driven technologies brought both new opportunities and problems. Intel started creating customized CPUs and accelerators intended to maximize AI workloads in response to these new demands.

The acquisition of Nervana Systems in 2016, a business that specialized in deep learning and neural network processors, was one of Intel's major forays into the AI field. Through this acquisition, Intel was able to accelerate its AI capabilities and incorporate Nervana's technology into its product range, marking a strategic shift towards artificial intelligence. Subsequently, the Intel Nervana Neural Network Processor (NNP) family was created to manage intricate AI workloads, providing data centers with great speed and scalability.

Apart from Nervana, Intel procured many firms, including as Mobileye, a technology company focused on autonomous driving, and Habana Labs, a producer of artificial intelligence processors. These acquisitions demonstrated Intel's dedication to growing its portfolio of AI products and improving its skills in edge computing, deep learning, and machine learning.

Arrow Lake and Future Prospects

As Intel continues to innovate in the AI arena, one of its most anticipated product lines is the Arrow Lake CPUs. Scheduled for launch in the fourth quarter of 2024, Arrow Lake represents a significant advancement in Intel's CPU technology, promising enhanced performance, power efficiency, and AI capabilities.

Features and Launch Plans for Arrow Lake CPUs

The Arrow Lake CPUs are expected to be built on Intel's advanced process technology, incorporating a combination of high-performance cores and energy-efficient cores. This hybrid architecture, first introduced with the Alder Lake series, allows for better optimization of workloads by dynamically allocating tasks to the appropriate cores. The high-performance cores handle demanding tasks such as gaming and content creation, while the energy-efficient cores manage background processes and less intensive applications, resulting in improved overall performance and power efficiency.

Key features of the Arrow Lake CPUs include:

Enhanced AI Capabilities: Arrow Lake CPUs are designed to integrate advanced AI accelerators, enabling faster and more efficient processing of AI workloads. This includes support for Intel's Deep Learning Boost (DL Boost) technology, which accelerates AI inference and training tasks.

Improved Graphics Performance: The integrated graphics in Arrow Lake CPUs are expected to deliver significant performance improvements, supporting high-resolution gaming, video editing, and other graphics-intensive applications.

Advanced Connectivity: Arrow Lake will support the latest connectivity standards, including PCIe 5.0 and DDR5 memory, ensuring compatibility with next-generation peripherals and delivering higher data transfer speeds.

Energy Efficiency: With a focus on reducing power consumption, Arrow Lake CPUs will incorporate advanced power management features, making them ideal for both desktop and mobile platforms.

Security Enhancements: Intel plans to include robust security features in Arrow Lake CPUs, protecting against various cyber threats and ensuring data integrity.

The launch of Arrow Lake is expected to bolster Intel's position in the CPU market, offering a compelling option for consumers and enterprises seeking high-performance computing solutions with advanced AI capabilities.

Patrick Gelsinger's Vision and Strategic Outlook

Since taking over as CEO of Intel in February 2021, Patrick Gelsinger has been instrumental in leading the firm to refocus on innovation and technological leadership. With extensive knowledge of Intel's past and culture, Gelsinger is a seasoned veteran of the semiconductor business and has presented a compelling future direction for the company.

Intel has started an ambitious plan to recover its competitive edge and spur growth in new industries, especially in AI and advanced computing, under Gelsinger's direction. His strategic vision includes some important projects:

Process Technology Leadership: Gelsinger has emphasized the importance of Intel reclaiming its position as a leader in semiconductor manufacturing. This includes accelerating the development of next-generation process technologies and ensuring that Intel's fabs (fabrication facilities) are among the most advanced in the world.

Expanding Foundry Services: To diversify its revenue streams, Intel has launched the Intel Foundry Services (IFS) initiative, offering its manufacturing capabilities to third-party customers. This move aims to capitalize on the growing demand for semiconductor manufacturing and position Intel as a key player in the global supply chain.

Innovation in AI and Quantum Computing: Gelsinger has prioritized investments in AI and quantum computing, recognizing their potential to drive future growth. Intel is focused on developing cutting-edge AI accelerators, neuromorphic computing technologies, and quantum processors, positioning itself at the forefront of these transformative fields.

Strengthening Partnerships and Ecosystems: Gelsinger believes in the power of collaboration and has sought to strengthen Intel's partnerships with technology companies, research institutions, and governments. By fostering a robust ecosystem, Intel aims to drive innovation and create new growth opportunities.

Cultural Transformation: Recognizing the need for cultural change within Intel, Gelsinger has advocated for a renewed emphasis on engineering excellence, agility, and customer-centricity. His leadership style emphasizes transparency, accountability, and a relentless focus on execution.

Intel's Competitive Strategy

As Intel navigates the competitive landscape, it faces formidable rivals in Nvidia and AMD, both of which have established strong footholds in the AI chip market. To effectively compete, Intel has adopted a multi-faceted strategy that leverages its strengths while addressing its weaknesses.

Intel's Approach to Competing with Nvidia and AMD

Product Innovation: Intel is committed to delivering cutting-edge products that meet the evolving needs of its customers. This includes not only CPUs but also a wide range of AI accelerators, GPUs, and specialized processors designed for specific applications. By continuously innovating and expanding its product portfolio, Intel aims to offer compelling alternatives to Nvidia and AMD's offerings.

Process Technology Advancements: Regaining leadership in process technology is a top priority for Intel. By accelerating the development and deployment of advanced manufacturing processes, Intel aims to produce more powerful and efficient chips, reducing the performance gap with its competitors.

Vertical Integration: Intel's vertically integrated model, which includes in-house design and manufacturing, provides a competitive advantage in terms of control over the supply chain and product optimization. This allows Intel to better align its products with customer needs and respond more quickly to market demands.

Strategic Acquisitions and Partnerships: Intel has strategically acquired companies like Habana Labs and Mobileye to bolster its AI and autonomous driving capabilities. Additionally, partnerships with industry leaders, research institutions, and cloud service providers enhance Intel's ecosystem and drive collaborative innovation.

AI Software and Frameworks: Intel recognizes the importance of a robust software ecosystem to support its hardware innovations. The company has invested in developing AI software tools and frameworks, such as the Intel oneAPI toolkit and OpenVINO, to simplify the deployment and optimization of AI workloads on Intel hardware.

Focus on Edge Computing: As the demand for edge computing grows, Intel is positioning itself as a key player in this space. By offering AI solutions that extend from the data center to the edge, Intel aims to capture new markets and provide comprehensive end-to-end solutions.

Innovations and Collaborations in AI Development

Intel's commitment to innovation and collaboration is evident in its approach to AI development. The company is investing heavily in research and development (R&D) to push the boundaries of what is possible with AI technology. Key areas of focus include:

Neuromorphic Computing: Intel is exploring neuromorphic computing, which mimics the human brain's neural architecture to achieve more efficient and powerful AI processing. The Intel Loihi research chip is a notable example, designed to handle complex, real-time AI tasks with minimal power consumption.

Quantum Computing: Intel is at the forefront of quantum computing research, aiming to develop quantum processors that can solve problems beyond the capabilities of classical computers. The company's efforts in quantum computing are complemented by its partnerships with leading research institutions.

Collaborations with Academia and Industry: Intel actively collaborates with academic institutions, industry partners, and research organizations to advance AI technology. These collaborations facilitate knowledge exchange, drive innovation, and accelerate the development of AI solutions.

OpenAI Partnership: Intel has partnered with OpenAI to leverage its deep learning expertise and develop AI solutions optimized for Intel hardware. This collaboration aims to enhance the performance and scalability of AI applications, benefiting a wide range of industries.

AI Ethics and Responsibility: Intel is committed to advancing AI responsibly and ethically. The company participates in initiatives and collaborates with stakeholders to address the ethical implications of AI and ensure that its technology is developed and used responsibly.

Intel's foray into the AI space is a calculated move toward embracing the direction of computing. Intel is in a strong position to use its resources and experience in the CPU business to further AI innovation. With the introduction of Arrow Lake CPUs, Intel has demonstrated its resolve to regain its technological leadership and successfully compete with Nvidia and AMD. This is further evidenced by

Patrick Gelsinger's strategic approach and visionary leadership. Utilizing consistent product innovation, progress in process technology, tactical acquisitions, and cooperative endeavors, Intel hopes to mold AI's future and hold its position as the world's foremost semiconductor company.

CHAPTER 5

THE TAIWANESE CONNECTION

Significance of Taiwan in the Tech Industry

Taiwan has long been acknowledged as a major player in the world of technology, especially when it comes to the production of semiconductors. Despite its limited geographic area, this island nation is essential to the worldwide supply chain for electronic components, especially chips and integrated circuits (ICs). A highly qualified workforce, strategic investments, and government policies all contribute to Taiwan's technical superiority.

The late 20th century saw Taiwan's government enact laws intended to promote industrial growth and technical innovation, which marked the beginning of the country's transformation into a global tech powerhouse. A notable achievement was the founding of the Hsinchu Science Park in 1980. Hsinchu, which was modeled after Silicon Valley, swiftly rose to prominence as a center for high-tech sectors, mainly semiconductor manufacturing. By drawing in large tech firms and fostering cooperation between government, business, and academia, the park fostered the development of a vibrant ecosystem for technological innovation.

The nation's emphasis on research and education has played a significant role in its technical leadership. Highly skilled engineers and scientists have been created in large quantities by Taiwan's research and academic institutions, including Academia Sinica and National Taiwan University. Additionally, by promoting an innovative and entrepreneurial culture, these institutions have helped to propel the tech industry forward.

Taiwan's Role as a Hub for Semiconductor Manufacturing

Taiwan's technological sector is anchored on its semiconductor industry, which is led by companies such as Taiwan Semiconductor Manufacturing Company (TSMC). TSMC is the largest dedicated independent semiconductor foundry in the world, having been established in 1987. It produces semiconductors for a wide range of uses, including high-performance computers, consumer electronics, and automobiles. Artificial intelligence is one of its most prominent markets.

The ability of TSMC to develop cutting-edge chips at scale and its sophisticated production procedures are the reasons behind its dominance in the semiconductor industry. The company's foundries are outfitted with state-of-the-art machinery, such as extreme ultraviolet (EUV) lithography, which facilitates the manufacturing of extraordinarily compact and potent chips. By consistently allocating resources into research and development, TSMC guarantees its position as a leader in semiconductor innovation.

Apart from TSMC, several other Taiwanese enterprises, including United Microelectronics Corporation (UMC) and MediaTek, have made noteworthy advancements in the worldwide semiconductor sector. Similar to TSMC, UMC offers foundry services and is a major player in the manufacturing of customized integrated circuits. In contrast, MediaTek is a well-known fabless semiconductor manufacturer that specializes in creating chips for mobile devices, wireless connectivity, and high-definition television.

Beyond the boundaries of the island, Taiwan's semiconductor sector is significant. Taiwanese chips are a major component of the global tech ecosystem and are essential to the operation of many different types of electronic gadgets. The COVID-19 epidemic brought this dependence to a sharp light, upending global supply chains and causing a global scarcity of semiconductors that impacted industries ranging from consumer electronics to automotive manufacturing.

Key Events and Trade Shows: Computex

An annual computer and technology trade expo called Computex Taipei is one of the most important events on Taiwan's tech calendar. Since its founding in 1981, Computex has expanded to rank among the biggest and most significant trade exhibitions worldwide, drawing innovators, industry leaders, and fans from all corners of the globe.

Computex provides a venue for businesses to present their most recent innovations and goods. It addresses several different subjects, such as blockchain, AI, IoT, 5G, and gaming. Keynote addresses, product debuts, and exhibits are all part of the event, which gives participants an inside look at the newest trends and advancements in the tech sector.

Computex has been instrumental in promoting international cooperation and showcasing Taiwan's technological prowess over the years. It gives Taiwanese businesses a platform to interact with clients, investors, and partners throughout the world. The occasion highlights Taiwan's role as a key participant in the global IT sector and highlights the nation's capacity for innovation and leadership across a range of technological fields.

Computex is more important than just commercial transactions. It also serves as a celebration of technology advancement and evidence of the group accomplishments of the worldwide IT community. The occasion encourages teamwork and knowledge exchange, propelling the sector forward and motivating the following wave of creatives.

Cultural and Familial Ties

Taiwan's tech sector is significant industrially, but it also has strong cultural and familial roots that have influenced its growth. The achievements of prominent figures in the sector, such as Jensen Huang of Nvidia and Lisa Su of AMD, are intricately linked to their Taiwanese origin, demonstrating the ways in which cultural influences may impact and propel scientific progress.

Taiwanese native Jensen Huang was a co-founder of Nvidia in 1993. Nvidia has emerged as a global leader in AI and graphics processing units (GPUs) under his direction. Huang's innovative mindset and imaginative approach have been crucial to Nvidia's success. Because of his propensity for spotting market trends and making strategic investments in emerging technology, Nvidia is leading the AI revolution.

Lisa Su, the CEO of AMD, is also of Taiwanese heritage. Despite her early relocation to the United

States, she has remained deeply connected to her Taiwanese roots, having been born in Tainan. Su's direction has revolutionized AMD, propelling the business's comeback and establishing it as a serious rival to Nvidia and Intel. AMD has reached new heights because to her concentration on engineering excellence and wise investments in cutting-edge technologies.

The Unique Connection Between Nvidia's Jensen Huang and AMD's Lisa Su

Beyond their common Taiwanese ancestry, Jensen Huang and Lisa Su have a deeper bond. Since the two are related, their separate positions in the tech business have an additional dimension. Since Jensen Huang's niece Lisa Su, their accomplishments in the tech industry are a fascinating family affair.

The tech community is intrigued and curious about this familial tie. Although each has forged its route and used unique tactics to bring their businesses to success, there is little doubt that their common history and family ties have shaped their leadership philosophies and methods for approaching innovation.

The experiences of Huang and Su demonstrate the usefulness of cultural values, familial support, and mentoring in developing effective leaders. Their accomplishments serve as an example of how people with comparable beginnings can succeed spectacularly in the global tech industry, inspiring many in Taiwan and beyond.

Impact of Their Leadership on Their Respective Companies

The leadership of Jensen Huang and Lisa Su has had a profound impact on their respective companies, Nvidia and AMD, shaping their trajectories and defining their roles in the tech industry.

Jensen Huang's Impact on Nvidia

Nvidia has grown from a specialized graphics card maker to a major player in artificial intelligence and high-performance computing under Jensen Huang's direction. Huang's idea on the future of computing, which is focused on GPUs and AI, has influenced Nvidia's product development and business approach.

Huang made a significant contribution when he realized that GPUs might be used for purposes other than gaming. He anticipated how GPUs will be useful for parallel computing, which is crucial for artificial intelligence and machine learning. This realization sparked the creation of CUDA, a parallel computing platform and programming style that is now a key component of Nvidia's artificial intelligence approach.

Huang has made sure that Nvidia remains ahead of the competition by placing a strong emphasis on research and development. The company's leadership in the AI chip market has been cemented by its ongoing investments in creating GPUs that are more potent and efficient. Products such as the Blackwell and the soon-to-be-released Rubin platform demonstrate Nvidia's dedication to advancing technological capabilities.

Huang has been instrumental in drawing top talent to Nvidia and establishing an innovative culture through his captivating leadership and ability to communicate a compelling future vision. His approach to leadership, which combines technical know-how with strategic vision, has been crucial in helping Nvidia navigate times of fast expansion and competitive challenges.

Lisa Su's Impact on AMD

Under Lisa Su's direction, AMD has undergone a radical change that has made it a powerful contender in the semiconductor market. In 2014, Su became CEO of AMD, which was having trouble competing. Her execution-focused approach and strategic vision have brought the organization back to life.

The creation and successful introduction of the EPYC server chips and Ryzen processors are two of Su's notable accomplishments. These products have not only eclipsed Intel's offerings in terms of efficiency and performance, but they have also closed the performance gap with Intel in many instances. AMD has once again become the market leader in CPUs thanks to Su's emphasis on performance and innovation.

Su places a high value on engineering excellence and has a customer-centric mindset in his leadership style. She has encouraged teamwork and accountability among AMD staff members, giving them the freedom to own their work and lead innovation. This culture change has been essential to AMD's transformation into a more competitive and nimble business.

Su's calculated bets on AI and high-end computing have put AMD in a strong position to take on Nvidia in the market for AI chips. The MI series accelerators and the company's dedication to an annual product cadence are examples of Su's forward-thinking strategy and her comprehension of the changing demands of the tech sector.

In summary

The Taiwanese connection in the tech industry is a complex phenomenon that includes the nation's position as a center for semiconductor manufacture, the importance of significant occasions such as Computex, and the cultural and family links that influence the leadership of notable firms such as Nvidia and AMD. Taiwan's innovative attitude, competent workforce, and smart investments have contributed to its technological success.

Jensen Huang and Lisa Su, who are both of Taiwanese origin, are prime examples of how family ties and cultural legacy can impact and propel technological innovation. Their individual contributions to AMD and Nvidia have had a significant influence on the global tech industry in addition to shaping the respective company trajectories.

The Taiwanese connection will continue to be vital to the growth and progress of semiconductor technology, even as the competition for supremacy in AI intensifies. Future generations might draw inspiration from Huang and Su's stories, which emphasize the value of vision, creativity, and leadership in succeeding in the ever-changing IT industry.

Chapter 6

THE MARKET DYNAMICS

Investor Reactions and Market Trends

The AI chip industry has become one of the most dynamic sectors within the technology landscape, capturing the attention of investors and market analysts alike. The strategic moves by industry giants like Nvidia, AMD, and Intel significantly influence investor sentiment and market trends, reflecting the broader implications for the tech economy.

Stock Market Responses to New Product Announcements

New product announcements from leading AI chip manufacturers are pivotal events that often cause significant shifts in stock prices. These announcements are meticulously planned to maximize impact, often coinciding with major tech events like Computex or company-specific showcases.

Nvidia: A Case Study

Nvidia's announcements, particularly those made by CEO Jensen Huang, are highly anticipated. For instance, when Nvidia unveiled its Rubin AI chip platform in 2026, the market responded with a notable uptick in Nvidia's stock price. This reaction was driven by several factors:

Technological Leadership: The Rubin platform, touted as the successor to the Blackwell chip, promised significant advancements in processing power and efficiency. This solidified Nvidia's position as a leader in AI chip technology.

Market Confidence: Investors have long viewed Nvidia as a reliable innovator. The announcement reinforced confidence in Nvidia's ability to maintain its competitive edge, driving stock prices higher.

AMD: Strategic Positioning

Similarly, AMD's product launches have a substantial impact on its stock performance. When AMD CEO Lisa Su introduced the MI325X accelerator, there was a positive market reaction, reflecting investor confidence in AMD's roadmap and its competitive positioning against Nvidia. The response was bolstered by:

Product Roadmap: AMD's clear and consistent roadmap, which includes the MI350 and MI400, provides a transparent view of the company's future, fostering investor trust.

Performance Metrics: AMD's focus on memory size, bandwidth, and computational performance in their announcements directly addresses key performance indicators valued by investors and industry analysts.

Intel: A Strategic Player

Intel's announcements, particularly those related to their Arrow Lake CPUs, also attract significant market attention. Intel's efforts to reassert its dominance in the AI and desktop CPU markets are closely watched. The stock market's reaction to Intel's announcements is often influenced by:

Market Catch-Up: Investors are keen to see whether Intel can close the gap with Nvidia and AMD in the AI chip sector.

Leadership Vision: CEO Patrick Gelsinger's strategic insights and future projections play a crucial role in shaping investor sentiment.

Analysis of Market Share and Sales Figures

Understanding the market dynamics in the AI chip sector requires a thorough analysis of market share and sales figures. These metrics provide a quantitative measure of each company's competitive position and growth trajectory.

Nvidia: The Dominant Force

Nvidia holds a commanding position in the AI semiconductor market, accounting for approximately 70% of AI chip sales. This dominance is attributed to several factors:

Technological Innovation: Nvidia's continuous innovation, exemplified by the Blackwell and Rubin platforms, has kept it at the forefront of the industry.

Strategic Partnerships: Collaborations with leading tech companies and data centers have expanded Nvidia's market reach and application base.

Nvidia's sales figures reflect its market leadership. For instance, the introduction of the Blackwell chip led to a significant increase in data center revenue, reinforcing its dominant market share. The anticipation of the Rubin platform is expected to further boost sales, as data centers and AI developers seek cutting-edge technology to support their growing needs.

AMD: A Rising Competitor

While Nvidia leads, AMD has been steadily increasing its market share. AMD's strategy focuses on:

Competitive Pricing: Offering high-performance AI chips at competitive prices has allowed AMD to capture a portion of the market traditionally dominated by Nvidia.

Innovation and Roadmap: The consistent rollout of new products, such as the MI300X, MI325X, and upcoming MI350 and MI400, positions AMD as a strong competitor.

AMD's sales figures show significant growth, particularly in sectors like gaming and data centers, where their GPUs and AI accelerators are gaining traction. This growth is a testament to AMD's effective market strategy and product innovation.

Intel: Reclaiming Ground

Intel's market share in the AI chip sector is smaller compared to Nvidia and AMD, but it remains a significant player due to its extensive history and technological capabilities. Intel's strategy involves:

Leverage Existing Strengths: Utilizing its expertise in CPU manufacturing to create AI-optimized processors like the Arrow Lake series.

R&D Investments: Heavy investments in research and development to innovate and compete in the AI space.

Intel's sales figures in the AI sector have been gradually improving as it rolls out new products and technologies. The Arrow Lake CPUs are expected to further enhance Intel's market presence, particularly in desktop applications and data centers.

Global Demand for AI Chips

The demand for AI chips has surged globally, driven by the rapid adoption of AI technologies across various industries. This demand is fueled by several key factors:

Generative AI Applications

The rise of generative AI applications, such as ChatGPT, DALL-E, and other AI-driven tools, has significantly increased the need for powerful AI chips. These applications require substantial computational power to process large datasets and generate high-quality outputs. As generative AI continues to evolve, the demand for advanced AI chips is expected to grow exponentially.

Data Center Needs

Data centers are the backbone of modern computing, providing the infrastructure necessary to support AI applications, cloud computing, and big data analytics. The increasing reliance on data centers for AI workloads has led to soaring demand for AI chips. Data centers require chips that offer:

High Computational Power: To handle complex AI algorithms and large-scale data processing.

Energy Efficiency: To reduce operational costs and environmental impact.

The expansion of data centers globally, particularly in regions like North America, Europe, and Asia, is driving the demand for AI chips. Companies are investing heavily in upgrading their data center capabilities to meet the growing needs of AI-driven applications.

Projections for Future Demand and Market Growth

The future demand for AI chips is poised to grow significantly, driven by advancements in AI technology and increasing adoption across various sectors. Several key trends and projections highlight this growth trajectory:

Continued Growth in AI Applications

As AI technologies become more sophisticated, their applications will expand into new areas such as healthcare, finance, autonomous vehicles, and smart cities. Each of these sectors will require specialized AI chips to handle specific workloads and applications, further driving demand.

Innovation in AI Chip Technology

Ongoing innovation in AI chip technology will play a crucial role in meeting future demand. Companies like Nvidia, AMD, and Intel are continually pushing the boundaries of what AI chips can achieve. Future advancements may include:

Enhanced Processing Capabilities: To support more complex AI models and larger datasets.

Improved Energy Efficiency: To reduce power consumption and operational costs in data centers.

Integration with Emerging Technologies: Such as quantum computing and neuromorphic computing, which could revolutionize AI processing.

Expanding Market for Edge AI

Edge AI, which involves processing AI workloads on local devices rather than centralized data centers, is an emerging trend that will drive demand for AI chips. Edge AI applications include:

IoT Devices: Smart home devices, industrial sensors, and wearable technology.

Autonomous Systems: Drones, robots, and autonomous vehicles that require real-time AI processing.

The growth of edge AI will create new opportunities for AI chip manufacturers, as these applications require chips that are optimized for performance, power efficiency, and compact form factors.

Global Market Projections

Analysts project robust growth in the global AI chip market over the next decade. Key projections include:

Market Size: The AI chip market is expected to reach several hundred billion dollars by the early 2030s, driven by the widespread adoption of AI technologies.

Annual Growth Rate: The market is projected to grow at a compound annual growth rate (CAGR) of approximately 20-30%, reflecting the increasing integration of AI across various sectors.

Regional Growth Patterns

Different regions will experience varying growth rates based on their technological infrastructure, investment in AI, and adoption rates:

North America: Expected to remain a leading market due to strong investment in AI research, robust technological infrastructure, and the presence of major tech companies.

Asia-Pacific: Anticipated to see significant growth, driven by rapid technological adoption, government initiatives, and expanding data center capabilities in countries like China, Japan, and South Korea.

Europe: Projected to experience steady growth, supported by investments in AI and digital transformation initiatives across various industries.

The complex interactions between investor mood, worldwide demand, and technological innovation affect the market dynamics of the AI chip sector. Nvidia, AMD, and Intel's strategic actions will have a big impact on market trends and competitive positioning as they continue to push the limits of AI chip technology. The rise in data center requirements and generative AI applications highlights the indispensable role of AI chips in contemporary computing, opening the door for further expansion and innovation in this exciting industry. In the upcoming years, the AI chip sector is expected to maintain its leadership position in technological innovation and economic expansion, as forecasts suggest strong demand and market expansion.

CHAPTER 7

TECHNOLOGICAL INNOVATIONS

Advancements in AI Chip Technology

The landscape of artificial intelligence (AI) chip technology has undergone significant transformation over the past decade. This chapter delves into the key technological breakthroughs by Nvidia, AMD, and Intel, exploring their impact on AI and computing, and projecting the future directions and emerging technologies that will shape the industry.

Key Technological Breakthroughs by Nvidia, AMD, and Intel

Nvidia

The Blackwell Architecture: The Blackwell architecture, which Nvidia unveiled in March 2024, attracted notice right away for being the "world's most powerful chip." The Blackwell chips' unmatched processing power and efficiency were highlighted in their specific design for data centers. Through the use of sophisticated graphics processing units (GPUs) tuned for AI workloads, the architecture processed data more quickly and effectively.

Rubin Platform: The Rubin platform, which is scheduled for release in 2026, is Nvidia's next big advancement in AI processor technology. The new GPUs from Rubin, along with the revolutionary Vera CPU and cutting-edge networking devices, were showcased by Nvidia CEO Jensen Huang. With its promise of even more computational power, economy, and versatility, the Rubin platform will undoubtedly represent a significant advancement in artificial intelligence and accelerated computing.

AI-Driven Innovations: AI progress has been greatly aided by Nvidia's GPUs. The organization's emphasis on optimizations unique to AI, including tensor cores for deep learning, has greatly improved the efficiency of AI models. With the release of the CUDA programming framework, developers were able to fully utilize GPUs for AI applications, which propelled Nvidia to the forefront of the industry.

AMD

The MI300X Accelerator: The 2023 release of AMD's MI300X marked a significant advancement in AI chip technology. The MI300X, well-known for leading the way in memory capacity, computation power, and inference performance, redefined the parameters for AI accelerators. It proved AMD's dedication to providing high-performance products designed with AI workloads in mind.

The MI325X and Future Roadmap: The MI325X accelerator, which CEO Lisa Su unveiled in Taipei, is scheduled for release in the fourth quarter of 2024. The MI350 for 2025 and the MI400 for 2026 are two products on AMD's roadmap that each promises small improvements in memory, bandwidth, and processing capacity. AMD's commitment to maintaining its leadership position in AI chip technology is demonstrated by its yearly release schedule for new product families.

Heterogeneous Computing: By combining CPUs and GPUs onto a single chip to improve performance and efficiency, AMD invented heterogeneous computing. This method makes it possible to handle a variety of workloads more successfully, especially in AI and machine learning. AMD's CPUs and GPUs work together to accelerate model training and data processing.

Intel

Arrow Lake CPUs: Intel's Arrow Lake CPUs, expected to launch in the fourth quarter of 2024, signify the company's aggressive push into AI and desktop computing. These CPUs incorporate advanced AI capabilities, offering improved performance and efficiency for AI applications.

Intel's focus on integrating AI features directly into their CPUs sets them apart in the market.

OneAPI and Software Innovations: Intel's OneAPI initiative aims to simplify the programming of diverse computing architectures, including CPUs, GPUs, and field-programmable gate arrays (FPGAs). This unified programming model enhances developer productivity and ensures optimal performance across different hardware platforms. Intel's emphasis on software innovations complements its hardware advancements.

AI-Powered Processors: Intel's Xeon processors have been enhanced with AI-specific features, such as deep learning boost (DL Boost) and hardware accelerators for neural networks. These enhancements enable faster inferencing and training of AI models, making Intel a strong contender in the AI chip market.

Future Directions and Emerging Technologies

Quantum Computing

Quantum computing represents a paradigm shift in computational power, offering the potential to solve complex problems beyond the reach of classical computers. Companies like Nvidia, AMD, and Intel are exploring quantum computing technologies to complement their AI chip offerings. Quantum computers can process vast amounts of data simultaneously, significantly accelerating AI computations and enabling breakthroughs in fields such as cryptography, drug discovery, and climate modeling.

Neuromorphic Computing

Neuromorphic computing aims to mimic the neural architecture of the human brain, offering energy-efficient and high-performance solutions for AI applications. Intel's Loihi chips are an example of neuromorphic processors designed to emulate the brain's synaptic activity. These chips excel at tasks such as pattern recognition and sensory processing, holding promise for future AI systems that require real-time and low-power computations.

Photonic Computing

Photonic computing leverages light instead of electrical signals to perform computations. This technology has the potential to revolutionize data processing by offering higher speeds and lower power consumption compared to traditional electronic chips. Companies are researching photonic circuits to enhance AI performance, particularly in data-intensive tasks like image and speech recognition.

Edge AI

Edge AI involves deploying AI models directly on edge devices, such as smartphones, IoT devices, and autonomous vehicles, rather than relying on cloud-based computations. This approach reduces latency, enhances privacy, and improves real-time decision-making capabilities. Nvidia's Jetson platform and Intel's Movidius chips are examples of edge AI solutions designed to bring AI capabilities to the edge.

Impact on AI and Computing

Accelerated AI Research and Development

Research and development in AI is reaching previously unheard-of levels thanks to Nvidia, AMD, and Intel's breakthroughs in chip technology. Researchers can train more sophisticated models more quickly and cheaply because to increased computing power. This acceleration encourages creativity in some AI-related subfields, such as reinforcement learning, computer vision, and natural language processing.

Democratization of AI

A wider spectrum of businesses and organisations are finding AI more accessible thanks to advancements in AI chip technology. AI gear has become more affordable and performs better, making it possible for research institutes and smaller businesses to take advantage of advanced AI capabilities. It is anticipated that the democratization of AI will promote economic growth and innovation in several industries.

Enhanced Performance and Efficiency

The most recent AI chips provide notable increases in both energy efficiency and performance. These improvements result in reduced operating costs and quicker processing times for data centers and AI-driven apps. Consequently, companies can implement additional AI solutions, boosting efficiency and opening up new use cases.

Real-Time AI Applications

Advances in AI chip technology are opening up new fields for real-time AI applications. Immediate data processing gives up new opportunities for AI-driven solutions, such as predictive maintenance, real-time language translation, and autonomous cars. These real-time applications have the power to change whole sectors of the economy and raise standards of living.

How These Advancements Will Shape the Future of AI and Computing

AI Integration in Everyday Life

AI will permeate daily life more and more as AI chips grow in strength and efficiency. Improved AI capabilities will aid wearables, smart home appliances, and personal assistants by providing more personalized and intuitive experiences. Smarter, more connected living spaces will result from the smooth incorporation of AI into everyday tasks.

Advancements in Healthcare

Healthcare is about to undergo a transformation thanks to AI-driven diagnostics and personalised therapy. Improved AI chips provide quicker and more precise medical data analysis, which results in early disease detection and customized treatment regimens. Predictive analytics, genomics, and imaging enabled by AI will revolutionize patient care and enhance results.

Autonomous Systems

The evolution of autonomous systems, such as robots, drones, and self-driving cars, depends on the creation of AI processors. For these systems to navigate complicated situations, real-time data processing and decision-making skills are essential. The introduction of autonomous systems will be accelerated by advancements in AI chip technology, improving efficiency and safety across a range of industries.

Smart Cities

AI chips will be essential to the creation of smart cities. Artificial intelligence (AI) technologies will make urban living more sustainable and efficient, enabling everything from energy optimization and traffic control to environmental monitoring and public safety. The quality of life for people living in cities will improve with the integration of AI chips into city infrastructure.

Industrial Automation

Automation powered by AI is being used by industries more and more to cut expenses and increase productivity. The implementation of smart factories, which can have autonomous machinery and systems that optimize production and minimize downtime, is made possible by advanced AI chips. Predictive maintenance enabled by AI will lower operational hazards and increase efficiency even more.

Education and Research

AI chips will transform research and education by offering cutting-edge tools for modeling, simulation, and data analysis. AI will be used by educational institutions to improve student engagement and personalize learning. Faster data processing and analysis will help researchers, hastening scientific advancements and discoveries.

Potential Applications and Industries Affected

Finance

The financial industry is leveraging AI for various applications, including algorithmic trading, fraud detection, and risk management. Advanced AI chips enable faster data analysis and decision-making, enhancing the accuracy and efficiency of financial operations. AI-driven insights will transform investment strategies and improve financial outcomes.

Healthcare

AI is transforming healthcare through improved diagnostics, personalized treatment plans, and predictive analytics. Enhanced AI chips enable faster and more accurate analysis of medical data, leading to better patient care. AI-powered imaging, genomics, and drug discovery will revolutionize the healthcare industry.

Automotive

The automotive industry is transforming with the development of autonomous vehicles. AI chips are crucial for real-time data processing and decision-making, enabling safe and efficient navigation. Advanced driver-assistance systems (ADAS) and self-driving cars will benefit from improved AI capabilities.

Retail

Retailers are adopting AI to enhance customer experiences, optimize supply chains, and improve inventory management. AI chips enable real-time data analysis and personalized recommendations, driving sales and customer satisfaction. The integration of AI in retail operations will streamline processes and reduce costs.

Manufacturing

Manufacturing is leveraging AI for automation, predictive maintenance, and quality control. Advanced AI chips facilitate the deployment of smart factories, where machines and systems operate autonomously. AI-driven insights will optimize production processes and improve efficiency.

Telecommunications

The telecommunications industry is using AI to enhance network management, optimize resource allocation, and improve customer service. AI chips enable real-time data analysis and decision-making, ensuring efficient and reliable network operations. AI-driven solutions will enhance connectivity and support the growth of IoT.

Agriculture

AI is transforming agriculture through precision farming, crop monitoring, and predictive analytics. Advanced AI chips enable real-time data analysis and decision-making, improving crop yields and resource efficiency. AI-driven insights will enhance food security and sustainability.

Energy

The energy sector is adopting AI to optimize production, distribution, and consumption. AI chips enable real-time data analysis and decision-making, improving efficiency and reducing costs. AI-driven solutions will enhance the reliability and sustainability of energy systems.

Entertainment

The entertainment industry is leveraging AI for content creation, recommendation systems, and immersive experiences. Advanced AI chips enable real-time data analysis and personalization, enhancing user experiences. AI-driven solutions will transform content production and consumption.

Transportation

AI is transforming transportation through enhanced logistics, route optimization, and autonomous vehicles. AI chips enable real-time data analysis and decision-making, improving efficiency and safety. AI-driven insights will enhance the reliability and sustainability of transportation systems.

Nvidia, AMD, and Intel's advances in AI chip technology are ushering in a new era of innovation and industry revolution. These innovations are opening up new use cases and prospects for AI systems in addition to improving their effectiveness and performance. AI chips will influence AI and computing in the future and present previously unimaginable opportunities for both society and technology as they develop further. These developments will have a profound effect, transforming entire industries and raising people's standard of living everywhere.

CHAPTER 8

CHALLENGES AND OPPORTUNITIES

Competitive Pressures

The top three companies in the semiconductor market—Intel, AMD, and Nvidia—compete fiercely with one another, particularly in the AI chip segment. Every business has different obstacles to overcome and uses various tactics to hold onto and increase its market share. Market demands, strategic objectives, and technology improvements all influence the competitive landscape.

Nvidia: The Market Leader

Nvidia has long been the dominant force in the AI chip market, thanks to its pioneering work in GPU technology. The company's GPUs are integral to AI and machine learning applications, offering unmatched performance and efficiency. Nvidia's success is rooted in its continuous innovation and ability to stay ahead of the competition. However, maintaining this leadership position is not without challenges.

Challenges:

Technological Advancement: Nvidia needs to consistently push the boundaries of technology to stay ahead. The launch of the Rubin platform, set to succeed the Blackwell chip, is part of this effort. However, developing cutting-edge technology requires substantial investment in research and development (R&D), which can strain financial resources.

Competition: AMD and Intel are intensifying their efforts to capture a larger share of the AI chip market. AMD's new AI processors and Intel's upcoming Arrow Lake CPUs are direct challenges to Nvidia's dominance. Nvidia must continuously innovate and release superior products to fend off these competitors.

Market Saturation: As the AI chip market grows, there is a risk of saturation. Nvidia must explore new applications and markets for its GPUs to sustain growth. This includes expanding beyond traditional data centers and exploring opportunities in automotive, healthcare, and other industries.

AMD: The Challenger

AMD has positioned itself as a formidable challenger to Nvidia. Historically known for its gaming GPUs, AMD has successfully transitioned into the AI chip market with products like the MI300X and the upcoming MI325X. AMD's strategy focuses on delivering high-performance, cost-effective solutions.

Challenges:

Brand Perception: While AMD has made significant strides, it still battles the perception that it is second to Nvidia in the AI space. Building a reputation for reliability and performance in AI applications is crucial for AMD's long-term success.

Innovation Pace: AMD must match or exceed Nvidia's pace of innovation. This involves substantial R&D investments and a robust product development pipeline. The planned annual release of new chip families (MI350 in 2025 and MI400 in 2026) demonstrates AMD's commitment, but execution will be key.

Strategic Partnerships: Forming strategic partnerships and securing design wins with major tech companies and data centers is essential. AMD needs to expand its ecosystem and ensure that its chips are widely adopted in AI applications.

Intel: The Veteran

Intel, a veteran in the semiconductor industry, has a strong legacy in CPU technology. However, its entry into the AI chip market with products like the Arrow Lake CPUs signifies its ambition to compete with Nvidia and AMD. Intel's extensive resources and experience are both an advantage and a challenge.

Challenges:

Market Entry: Intel is relatively new to the AI chip market compared to Nvidia and AMD. Establishing a foothold requires significant marketing efforts and proof of performance. Intel must demonstrate that its products can compete on par or better with those from Nvidia and AMD.

Technological Transition: Transitioning from traditional CPUs to AI-optimized chips involves overcoming significant technological hurdles. Intel must ensure that its new products meet the high-performance standards required for AI applications.

Integration with Existing Ecosystems: Intel needs to ensure that its AI chips integrate seamlessly with existing hardware and software ecosystems. This requires close collaboration with developers and industry partners to optimize performance and compatibility.

Regulatory and Supply Chain Issues

The dynamics of supply chains and international trade regulations have a significant impact on the semiconductor sector. Production, distribution, and the general stability of the market can all be significantly impacted by changes in regulations and supply chain disruptions. It is a challenge for Nvidia, AMD, and Intel to negotiate these complications and continue to grow steadily.

Impact of Global Trade Policies

Global trade policies can significantly affect the semiconductor industry. Tariffs, export controls, and trade agreements shape the flow of raw materials and finished products across borders. Recent geopolitical tensions, especially between the United States and China, have introduced new challenges.

Key Issues:

Tariffs and Export Controls: The imposition of tariffs on semiconductor components and the implementation of export controls can increase costs and disrupt supply chains. For example, the U.S. has imposed export controls on certain high-tech components to China, impacting companies that rely on Chinese manufacturing capabilities.

Trade Agreements: Trade agreements between countries can either facilitate or hinder the flow of semiconductor products. Agreements that promote free trade and reduce tariffs are beneficial, while restrictive agreements can pose challenges.

Regulatory Compliance: Companies must navigate a complex web of regulations in different countries. Compliance with environmental regulations, labor laws, and intellectual property protections adds layers of complexity to operations.

Supply Chain Disruptions

The semiconductor supply chain is intricate and global, involving multiple stages from raw material extraction to chip fabrication and assembly. Disruptions at any stage can have ripple effects across the industry.

Key Issues:

Raw Material Shortages: The semiconductor industry relies on rare and specialized materials, such as silicon, cobalt, and rare earth elements. Shortages of these materials can delay production and increase costs.

Manufacturing Bottlenecks: Semiconductor fabrication plants (fabs) require significant capital investment and time to build. Any delays or capacity constraints at fabs can slow down the entire supply chain. The COVID-19 pandemic highlighted these vulnerabilities, leading to widespread chip shortages.

Logistics and Transportation: Efficient logistics and transportation are crucial for the timely delivery of components. Disruptions in shipping routes, port closures, and transportation delays can impact the supply chain.

Strategies for Mitigating Risks and Ensuring Stability

To navigate regulatory and supply chain challenges, Nvidia, AMD, and Intel employ various strategies to mitigate risks and ensure stability.

Nvidia:

Diversifying Supply Chains: Nvidia diversifies its supply chain to reduce dependency on any single region or supplier. By establishing relationships with multiple suppliers across different geographies, Nvidia can mitigate the impact of regional disruptions.

Investing in Local Manufacturing: Nvidia invests in local manufacturing capabilities to reduce reliance on international supply chains. This includes partnerships with local fabs and exploring opportunities for in-house production.

Regulatory Advocacy: Nvidia actively engages with policymakers to advocate for favorable trade policies and regulations. By participating in industry associations and lobbying efforts, Nvidia aims to influence policies that support the semiconductor industry.

AMD:

Strategic Partnerships: AMD forms strategic partnerships with key suppliers and manufacturers to secure a stable supply of critical components. These partnerships often involve long-term agreements that ensure priority access to materials and production capacity.

Supply Chain Transparency: AMD invests in supply chain transparency initiatives to identify and address potential risks early. By monitoring supplier performance and conducting regular audits, AMD can proactively manage disruptions.

Resilient Design: AMD designs its chips with resilience in mind, ensuring that they can be manufactured using alternative materials or processes if necessary. This flexibility helps mitigate the impact of material shortages or manufacturing bottlenecks.

Intel:

Vertical Integration: Intel leverages its vertical integration strategy to control more stages of the supply chain. By owning and operating its fabs, Intel reduces dependency on external manufacturers and can better manage production capacity.

Global Manufacturing Footprint: Intel expands its global manufacturing footprint to reduce regional risks. With fabs in multiple countries, Intel can shift production in response to regional disruptions or regulatory changes.

Collaborative Ecosystems: Intel collaborates with industry partners, including governments and other tech companies, to build resilient ecosystems. These collaborations focus on shared resources, joint R&D efforts, and coordinated responses to supply chain challenges.

In summary

The market for AI chips faces intense competition and regulatory obstacles. Nvidia, AMD, and Intel have to negotiate a complex world of technical advancement, competitive markets, and international trade laws. These businesses work to keep their top spots and profit from the growing market for AI chips by implementing strategic measures to reduce risks and guarantee stability.

Computing's future will be shaped by the actions and choices made by these industrial titans as the AI chip race proceeds. Their performance in this high-stakes battle will depend on their capacity for innovation, regulatory change adaptation, and robust supply chain building. The progress of AI technology will be driven by the dynamic interaction between collaboration and competition, which will ultimately redefine the limits of what is possible in the digital age.

CONCLUSION

THE FUTURE OF AI CHIPS

Predictions for the Next Decade in AI Chip Development

The next decade in AI chip development is poised to be transformative, characterized by rapid advancements and significant innovations. These advancements will not only enhance the capabilities of AI systems but also redefine the landscape of technology and society.

Enhanced Performance and Efficiency

One of the primary areas of focus will be on improving the performance and efficiency of AI chips. Nvidia's Rubin platform, AMD's MI325X, and Intel's Arrow Lake are just the beginning. Future AI chips will likely incorporate:

Advanced Architectures: Chips will adopt more sophisticated architectures, leveraging quantum computing principles and neuromorphic designs to achieve unprecedented processing power and efficiency.

Increased Parallelism: Greater parallelism in GPU and CPU designs will allow for more simultaneous computations, dramatically speeding up AI tasks.

Energy Efficiency: As the demand for AI computation grows, so will the need for energy-efficient solutions. Innovations such as better thermal management, low-power transistors, and energy-efficient AI algorithms will be crucial.

Integration of AI Capabilities Across Devices

AI chips will become ubiquitous, integrated across a wide range of devices beyond data centers and high-performance computing systems. This will include:

Edge Computing Devices: AI chips will be embedded in edge devices, enabling real-time data processing and decision-making in IoT devices, autonomous vehicles, and smart home systems.

Consumer Electronics: Smartphones, laptops, and wearables will feature advanced AI capabilities, offering personalized experiences and improved functionality.

Expansion of AI Applications

The scope of AI applications will expand significantly, driven by the capabilities of next-generation AI chips:

Healthcare: AI will revolutionize diagnostics, personalized medicine, and drug discovery, powered by advanced AI chips capable of processing vast amounts of medical data.

Finance: Financial services will leverage AI for fraud detection, algorithmic trading, and risk management, utilizing the enhanced analytical capabilities of AI chips.

Manufacturing: AI-driven automation and predictive maintenance will become standard in manufacturing, improving efficiency and reducing downtime.

Advances in Networking and Connectivity

AI chips will play a crucial role in advancing networking and connectivity technologies:

5G and Beyond: The integration of AI chips in communication networks will optimize data flow and enhance the performance of 5G and future 6G networks.

Network Security: AI-driven security measures will protect against cyber threats, leveraging the real-time processing power of AI chips to detect and respond to anomalies.

Long-Term Impact on Technology and Society

The long-term impact of AI chips on technology and society will be profound, influencing various aspects of daily life, economic structures, and ethical considerations.

Economic Transformation

AI chips will drive economic growth and transformation:

Job Creation and Displacement: While AI and automation will create new job opportunities in tech and related fields, they will also displace traditional roles, necessitating reskilling and education programs.

Industry Disruption: Entire industries will transform, with companies that leverage AI gaining a competitive edge. This will lead to the emergence of new business models and economic ecosystems.

Societal Changes

The integration of AI chips into everyday life will bring about significant societal changes:

Improved Quality of Life: AI-driven innovations in healthcare, transportation, and personal devices will improve the quality of life, offering better health outcomes, safer travel, and enhanced convenience.

Digital Divide: The proliferation of AI technologies may exacerbate the digital divide, with access to advanced AI tools and devices becoming a marker of socio-economic status. Addressing this divide will be crucial to ensure equitable benefits from AI advancements.

Ethical and Privacy Concerns

The rise of AI chips will also raise ethical and privacy concerns:

Data Privacy: The vast amounts of data processed by AI chips will necessitate robust data privacy measures to protect individual information.

Bias and Fairness: Ensuring that AI systems are fair and unbiased will be a critical challenge, requiring continuous monitoring and improvement of AI algorithms and the data they use.

Autonomy and Control: As AI systems become more autonomous, questions about human oversight, control, and accountability will become increasingly important.

Final Thoughts

More than just a business rivalry, the battle between Nvidia, AMD, and Intel to create the most sophisticated AI chips propels advancements in technology. All company's innovations push the envelope of what's feasible, resulting in discoveries that help the whole tech industry as well as society at large.

Artificial intelligence chip developments are not taking place in a vacuum. They are a component of a broader trend in computing convergence where powerful, networked systems are created by combining AI, quantum computing, and sophisticated networking. New opportunities will become available as a result of this convergence, including complex simulations and real-time AI applications.

While Nvidia, AMD, and Intel's competitive dynamics are significant, cooperation will be essential to the advancement of AI technology. To address the difficult problems that lie ahead and make sure that the advantages of artificial intelligence (AI) are widely distributed, collaborations between tech companies, academic institutions, and governments will be crucial.

Summary of Key Points

Enhanced Performance and Efficiency: Future AI chips will feature advanced architectures, increased parallelism, and energy-efficient designs, leading to significant performance improvements.

Integration Across Devices: AI chips will be integrated into a wide range of devices, from edge computing systems to consumer electronics, expanding the reach of AI.

Expansion of AI Applications: AI applications will proliferate across various sectors, including healthcare, finance, and manufacturing, driven by the capabilities of next-generation AI chips.

Advances in Networking and Connectivity: AI chips will enhance networking technologies, improving data flow and security in 5G and future networks.

Economic Transformation: AI chips will drive economic growth, create new job opportunities, and disrupt traditional industries, leading to new business models.

Societal Changes: AI-driven innovations will improve quality of life but may also exacerbate the digital divide, necessitating measures to ensure equitable access to AI benefits.

Ethical and Privacy Concerns: The rise of AI chips will raise ethical issues related to data privacy, bias, fairness, and autonomy, requiring ongoing attention and regulation.

Reflection on the Ongoing Race and Its Broader Implications

The constant competition between Nvidia, AMD, and Intel is evidence of the IT industry's unrelenting pace of innovation. Because of this competition, every company is forced to push the boundaries of what is feasible, leading to quick innovations that benefit society and the IT community as a whole in addition to their bottom lines.

But there are difficulties in this race. Companies have to navigate complicated technical, ethical, and regulatory landscapes because of the high risks. As these companies progress, striking a balance between the necessity for innovation and concerns about privacy, equity, and social effect will be essential.

This contest has wider ramifications than just the tech sector. AI chips will have an impact on society, the economy, and even geopolitics as they are more incorporated into daily life. Leaders in AI chip development will have a strategic edge that affects economic competitiveness and global power dynamics.

Furthermore, the advancement of AI chips emphasizes Taiwan's significance in the global supply chain for technology. Taiwan is an essential player in the development of AI technology, serving as the venue for important occasions such as Computex and housing significant semiconductor manufacturers. Maintaining the security and stability of this supply chain is essential to the AI chip industry's future development and innovation.

To sum up, AI chips have a bright future ahead of them and can significantly progress both technology and society. However, achieving this potential will need a well-rounded strategy that takes into account social and ethical ramifications in addition to technological and financial considerations. The competition between Nvidia, AMD, and Intel is a microcosm of the larger difficulties and possibilities that the tech sector must overcome to successfully negotiate the complexity of the AI-driven future.

Made in the USA
Las Vegas, NV
14 November 2024